WORDWAVES

Wordwaves Copyright © 2022 Barwarre Poets

All rights reserved. This book is copyright. Copyright for each individual piece of writing, illustrations and photography remains with the individual author. Except for private study, research, criticism or reviews, as permitted under the Copyright Act, no part of this book may be reproduced by any process without the written permission of the publishers.

Published by Jaymah
Edited by the authors
Illustrations by Geraldine Foley
Photography by Tom Adair, Sheila Swanborough, Helen Cox
Cover Design by Nathan Adair

ISBN: 978-0-6453770-3-3

Introduction

Words	**Waves**
dancing	swelling
rhyming	rolling
singing	spilling
shouting	cleansing
flying	wearing
weird	wild

connecting

Wordwaves
wash over, wash away, wash clean

Wordwaves
enlighten, invigorate, enlarge

Wordwaves
weave images, connections, meanings, community

Welcome to **Wordwaves**

There are many people who are fans of all forms of the arts in the village at Barwarre Gardens. So many readers and writers. So many who have been teachers of English and literature. So many who have been actors, artists and sculptors. So many singers and musicians. Barwarre is a thriving artistic haven.

Poetry began with a little group writing Australian bush poetry, flourishing over months of Covid lockdown. Then Tom Adair had the idea of a broader focus for poetry and immediately people jumped on board. Today we have five poets who have penned the book you are about to read. In alphabetical order they are Tom Adair, Helen Cox, Geraldine Foley, Nancy Leslie and Sheila Swanborough.

Tom Adair is a retired teacher who loves playing with words, meaning and form.

Helen Cox is a nurse and academic who is a published author and an aspiring poet.

Geraldine Foley is a retired librarian who has worked in special and educational libraries. She is also a retired teacher.

Nancy Leslie has been a farmer and has co-authored histories of two Victorian towns. She is new to writing poetry.

Sheila Swanborough has worn many hats in her lifetime but has always enjoyed writing, especially narrative poetry. Sheila was the first Barwarre Bush Bard.

Poems are presented alphabetically by title or first line.

Written and produced on
Wadawurrung land that was never ceded.

TABLE OF CONTENTS

An Easter Meditation	11
A Stroll Around the Gardens	13
Clouds	14
Cold Mornings	15
Cold Sunday	16
Collaboration	17
Craft	18
Creeping Covid	19
Dancing	20
Death of the Author	21
Brazilian Embroidery Lessons	22
Dinner Last Night	23
Doing the Crossword with Joan	24
Eddy	25
Ennui	26
Even a Brick Wants to be Something	27
Excuse Me, Sir	28
For the Love of Rhythm	29
Gardening by the Seat of My Pants	30
Grandma's Wishes	31
Greet the Day	31
Haiku	32
Healing	34
Henry the Hungry Huntsman	36
Homeless	38

I was Autumn Once	40
Just a Thought	42
Memories of My Dad	42
Marlene	44
Medical Profession	45
Milk	46
Mother's Driving Adventures	47
My Friend has Gone	50
My Guts are Gone	51
My New Chair	55
My Sewing Machine and Me	56
Naming Baby	59
Niente (Nothing)	60
October	62
Pebbles	63
Relief	66
Rural Women's Network	67
Seasons Come...	69
So, what Now...?	70
Song for Ukraine	72

The Book	74
The Drop Spider	76
The Literature Festival	78
The Lobby	79
The Mall Rats	80
The Room Belonged to Daisy	83
The September Quake	84
The WWW	86
There's a Gathering Sadness	87
The Times They are A-Changin'	88
This Way or That	92
Today	93
Trying Day	94
Village Life	96
Violence	97
Voice in Tribute	99
Water Runs Downhill - Part 1	103
Water Runs Downhill - Part 2	105
Who Am I?	106
World Poetry Day	107
Yesterday	109

WORDWAVES

An Easter Meditation

My world seemed sad, abandoned
All around was destruction, devastation,
young lives wasted, death.
I asked, "God where are you, do you care?"
There came a voice deep in my spirit
"Be still… watch… listen."

I walked in the forest, I saw decay, dead leaves, broken branches.
Again I asked, "Where are you God?"
Then I heard the song of birds
flying free,
I saw burrowing creatures making homes in the leaves,
Insects scurrying past, a delicate flower hidden in the undergrowth.
And I saw there the hand of God.

I roamed a lonely seashore, felt the rush of the wind.
Saw empty seashells that once held life, flotsam washed up, abandoned.
"Are you here too, God?"
The beach pebbles showed his hand, smoothed, refined, polished
 by the waves.
I saw that same hand at work in my life.
I saw his love as endless as the sea, as boundless as the sky.

I looked again in the city streets, searching, seeking God.
With new eyes I saw lives mended, healed, hearts set free.
People caring, reaching out with the hands of love,
I heard voices filled with peace and I saw God in it all.

Sheila

BARWARRE POETS

A Stroll Around the Gardens

Everyone is out it seems
Chairs on front porches
People stopping to chat
.... No reason to be lonely.

The gardens are lovely
Everyone seems to care
About how they look
.... No reason to be dreary.

My front is on the south side
No sun and often cool
So I walk around and say g'day
.... No reason to be teary.

Warm hearted people everywhere
I am so glad I came
I'm settled and I'm quite involved
.... Every reason to be happy.

Helen

Clouds

I am made by invisible forces
I cannot control what I'll be
My spirit is joyful but you'd never know
Because you'll never see the real me.

On fine days I create little daydreams
For lovers on grass gazing up
A horse maybe, with a rider
Or a tree or even a pup.

People smile when I'm all white and fluffy
days for picnics or a stroll on the shore
and when the gold sun reflects its light through me
hearts lift and I fluff even more.

But I can turn in a moment, become moody
I will thunder, send rain lashing down
causing floods, felling trees, wreaking havoc
widespread ruin where there once was a town.

So I am happy, broody, angry and worse
A kind of schizoid messy recipe
Poor little cloud drifting sad and forlorn
I think I'm in need of some therapy.

Helen

Cold Mornings

Icy morning frost heralds a bright sunny day
Energising, happy making, light of heart
and foot.

Grey drizzle, arctic blast right through your coat
Fingers numb, nose red, eyes smart
Cold through.

Wind is fierce in winter, not the gentle breeze
of summer, or spring, soft against your face.
Just gales.

Do I wish the winter gone? Frost, gales and
lashing rain? But counter that with soup, and open fires
And a good book. Ah!

Helen

Cold Sunday

The wind is whistling around the door
And it feels so cold and drear
There's a wintry sunshine but my heart's sore
For the one I held so dear

I could sit and weep but what's the use
It's time to shake my bones
Get out of the house, stop being a goose
Stop the sorry overtones

It's all about resilience
Finding courage to face the new day
Hold memories dear but have the sense
To know I will find the way

Tomorrow holds promise anew
And the night was not so bad
The dreams are now fading and few
And I find myself less sad

Good friends seem to be the key
Deep talks, and then some fun
Room some days to let me be
But others to get out in the sun

And I have good mates aplenty
To help me through the day
I counted up to more than twenty
Thank God for them I say

Helen

Collaboration

Note: I was walking up to the Centre and this old primary school ditty for remembering pronouns was in my head along with the covid we're all in this together messages we hear from the media, so I decided to use it to describe everything as interconnected planetary things. I rhymed the second and fourth lines which seems to be my favourite.

I, me, he, she, it
No matter what the weather
We, us, they, them, you
We're all in this together

Not an adjective in sight
It's plainspeak kind of talking
We're all cut from the same cloth
So let's get relations working

No one's better or more important
We just need to do our best
To get on, not fight, there is no war
Just humankind and all the rest

Across race, religion and colour
Let's meet in real humility
And tend the trees and birds and mountains
To the best of our ability

I, me, he, she, it
No matter what the weather
We, us, they, them, you
We're all in this together

Helen

Craft

Making craft I'm in a mess, linen, cotton, woollen dress
Every surface untidily covered, delicate fabric, this takes over
Paper, ruler, crafts galore, in the drawers there's such a store
Partner frowns, he's not so sure, tidy up, that is the law
Bathroom laundry not in there. If I don't do it, it could be war.

Paste and paint, tidy no, where to store it, that's the go
Could be in a sizeable shed, this solution not a resolution.
Now my partner seeing red, you should hear what he said!
Without craft it brings me low, with it, now see me grow.
Making craft it soothes me so, please please let me sew.

Nancy

Creeping Covid

It lurks in quiet places
In corridors, behind the door
It might be in the aircon duct
Or slipped down beneath the floor

That spiky ball of Covid
Is pulsing red and throbby
Pouncing on the unaware
Until they feel quite wobbly

It has reached Barwon Heads I hear
And the MCG's a hot spot
And Geelong I know were playing there
So its bound to grow a lot

I am feeling a little anxious now
might come into my back yard
Should I jab? I've got history
So I must be on my guard

Looks like it'll never go away
And we need to learn to cope
A yearly threat to our wellbeing
but a jab will bring us hope.

Helen

Dancing

With personality so mild, Grandma loves her clever child
On ballet toes moving swiftly, technique is right and so nifty
She's tall for her age, is she right for the stage?
Running fast and so nimble, now she turns on a thimble.
Examiner so serious and now grandma is almost delirious.
The music crescendo loud, highly paid pianist so skilled
The attentive audience feels quite thrilled.
Graceful gliding now you see, ballet students sway like trees.
Reaching up on her toes high, into the finale, into the light.
Holding her curtsey the end of the night.
Grandma's satisfied, feeling alright.

Nancy

Death of the Author

I have read all the 'Sister' books to date
Lucinda Riley is the writer
the Pleiades girls, their pasts, their fate
whose stars keep shining brighter

I finished the seventh book last night
It left me quite deflated
I expected answers to their plight
But curiosity was unsated

There's a final book that's still to come
Lucinda promised will answer questions
But today I am just struck dumb
It's not going to come, is the suggestion

Because…

The much-loved author died last week,
no final book from Riley
Unless there's stuff in the bottom drawer
That last book seems unlikely

Helen

Brazilian Embroidery Lessons

Take a piece of silken thread
Sharp needle, rude word said.
Needle threader such a help
But it breaks our silken thread.
Knots are frayed and awfully twisted
All so very inconvenient.
Delma teaches us much more
Till my head is very sore.
Patience now, you'll get the swing
Soon your thread will really sing.
Practice, practice, golden rule
Till you're perfect, like old school.
Alternating satin stitch
Really tends to make me itch.
International Brazilian daisy
Leaves, rolled roses, not too lazy.
Try again, no - get it right
In the fabric, a longer bite.
Thread names, Iris, Lola, Nova
Colour numbers, knock me over.

Delma's lessons, good content
Soon we feel encouragement.
Centre fine 'fine growth' as you please
House work forgotten, in dust we sneeze.
Pistol stitch, you'll want to switch it
Bullion, French knots, till you ditch it.
Now wait, don't be so pained
For dear teacher will explain.
Up ahead will come success
Dainty flowers will express.
Artistic pictures, great results
Not one stitch will be at fault.

Nancy

Dinner Last Night

This is about a dinner with Helen and Glenn Powers to celebrate the team we had created before Glenn stepped down as Chair of the Residents Association Committee.

Out to dinner with friends last night
Fine service wine and food
Shared stories, lots of laughter
And a light-hearted kind of mood.

It was a little thank you meal
For a job we did together
A team that worked so smoothly
Through all kinds of weather.

We've now passed it on to others
Who'll be working hard for all
We hope that they enjoy the task
And never drop the ball.

Helen

Doing the Crossword with Joan

It's like a little ritual
Those days up by the fire
If someone gets there before me
I'm disappointed but its not dire.

There is only one paper I like
The Age, so that I find
And we settle in to work it out
To exercise our mind.

We work our way through most
Before we turn to Dan
Our trusty mobiles find his site
And to cheat we ask our man.

It's Joan and me up by the fire
Our little crossword task
and when we get it as mostly we do
in our cleverness we bask.

Helen

Eddy

I visited my brother yesterday.
He is in a home for the aged.
His name is Edward, although on his door it says 'Eddy'.
The cleaner calls, "Eddy, I'm cleaning your room now."

I don't like this 'Eddy".
I feel it reeks of the larrikin.
Full of generous bravado.
A name with large stories of little substance.

He wants the address of the mansion we had.
Does he mean my grandmother's house?
Yet his description of where he is,
"Pentridge, without the guns," is reasonably accurate.
He asks me to get him out.

We go for an hour.

To a pub for a glass of wine and a bowl of chips
and a television with the Boxing Day Test.
He boasts of centuries, leg spinners and hat tricks.
Of being able to beat me at tennis, left handed with a frying pan.

It is time to go back.
As we near his 'jail'
I hear him sigh heavily and say, "That's life".
Followed by, "You know I'm 80 next year."

"We'll have a big party EDDY," I reply.

Geraldine

Ennui

Ennui
I love the word.
French
and different in sound to boredom
yet equal in its depth.

Geraldine

WORDWAVES

Even a Brick Wants to be Something

I was panicked about having to produce a poem by the next meeting of the Barwarre Poetry Group. I mentioned this to a dear friend who sent me a link to the American Poet Laureate, Billy Collins. Not a rhyme in sight! The next evening, I was watching a movie and the male role, after a deeply sad and poignant part of his life and with fear and trepidation returned to lecture in Architecture. He held a brick in his hand and opened his lecture with, "Even a brick wants to be something!" There was my beginning. Two days later I passed the Flying Brick Cider Co. There was my end.

EVEN A BRICK WANTS TO BE SOMETHING

A TOWER STRONG IN ITS VIGIL

A MOAT TO KEEP THE DISTANCE

A BRIDGE TO CONNECT

A HOUSE WITH WINDOWS AND TREES

AND A CHIMNEY

EVEN A BRICK WANTS TO BE SOMETHING

...MAYBE IT CAN FLY

Geraldine

Barwarre Poets

Excuse Me, Sir

Excuse me sir, have you seen my mother?
No, not Herbaceous, he's my brother.
My Mum is grungy, green and yellow
and you look like such a kind fellow.

She said she was going to the shops
and would be back with some chops.
I am really sick with worry
because she seemed in a terrible hurry.

"I have to get away", I heard her mutter
as she pushed me into the gutter.
I know I have been naughty and bad
but I am very sorry and very sad.

I didn't really mean to bite off her peg
but she has seven other legs.
Gee, Sir, I was just having some fun,
(but it did taste good with sauce on a bun).

I hope you are not trying to hide her
I tell you I am just a poor innocent spider.
I know I said I'd bite her bum
but come on, that would be dumb.

Her bum is putrid, horrid and smelly
but, oh yum, that big lovely belly.
I don't really mean that Sir,
I just need your help to find her.

You can? oh, that is great,
now I can release all my hate.
Oops, did I say that?
I wanted to keep that under my hat.

Look at my innocent eyes, all eight,
How can such a cute spider hate?
Hot revenge is not my style
I am patient and will wait a while.

Tom

For the Love of Rhythm

I have always loved the sound of drums
Strong rhythms stir down deeply
in my body a wild beat thrums
and I am caught completely

Seven minutes of Bolero on bongo
Or O'Carolan on the bodhran beating
African drums sound like the Congo
Continents in sound are meeting

Percussion in the orchestra
Leads the way with rhythms clever
The strings and woodwinds fall into line
As the drums hold it all together

I wish I was a drummer bold
Though both bodhran and bongos I play
A full drum kit would be solid gold
I could bang away all day

Small addendum. I now have a drum kit!

Helen

Gardening by the Seat of My Pants

A quick trip to Bunnings and home with some plants
Some Pumpkin, Coriander, Bok Choy,
Some shrubs for the front with colour and style
But open gardens? Well I'm a bit coy.

I put them all out where they were going to live
And just chatted with them for a day
And then with sun, mild breeze and blue skies
I settled them in where they'll stay

I am a bit of a green thumb just like my dad
Most things will grow and do well
What I lack though is imagination
What goes where, like I wove a spell..

..to make it look magical, I so wish I could
A lush rich nirvana of plants
But I muddle along as best I can
Called 'Gardening by the Seat of My Pants.'

Helen

Grandma's Wishes

Wishes won't avoid calamity; there is great need for sanity.
Best foot forward, individual will, family traditions holding still.
Set sights high for an example, good training proves more than ample.
The way to go not in the sand, but much higher on mountain land.
A level head will see you through. You will find the Bible true.

Nancy

Greet the Day

Waking slowly and after a yawn
Think carefully, what you'll do with this morn
Now out of this warm cosy bower
Your body's expecting to gain full power
So swing out of bed and head for the shower

After some food you're ready for work
So get stuck into this and don't shirk.
Later, work permitting, there'll be time for fun
Pay no attention if you're lacking the sun.
Work, exercise, play games and run.
You're not being chased, the day has begun.

Plan to make contact with somebody nice
Plan ahead for a taste of cake and spice
Don't stand around, seize this wonderful day
This life belongs to you, now play

Kick up your heels, you can't help but win
Play some good music, now you can sing
If you sing flat it's OK, with plenty of zing
Now you're feeling good, spirit floats on the wing.
Take up the cow bell and ring it like hell.

Now the day's ended, you'd like to thank God
After all He's the one who gave you the nod.
Thank Him now, you're safe in your home.
Isn't it lovely, your own special abode?

Such a great place, your very own space
Think, contemplate, of your life, it's so ace.
Now pray and sleep soundly, you've nothing to fear.
You can dream sweetly, as God has your ear.

Nancy

Haiku

Haiku is a three-line, beautifully descriptive, form of poetry. If read in Japanese, most traditional haiku would have five syllables, or sounds, in the first line, seven in the second, and five in the last. The traditional philosophy of haiku includes the focus on a brief moment in time; the use of provocative, colourful images; an ability to be read in one breath; and a sense of sudden enlightenment and illumination.

The poem gains its energy by the intuitive or emotional leap that occurs in the space between the poem's two parts, creating a gap and unexpected relationship, between the first two lines and the third. The art of haiku lies in creating exactly that gap, in leaving something out, and in dwelling in the cut that divides the haiku into its two energizing parts.

Wordwaves

A cone on his head
Protects the newly spayed wound
Still a sloppy grin.

Baby belly swell
Young mother gently waiting
Life-long love ahead.

Splashing through puddles
Gum boots, laughing faces
Tired mother snaps.

Sunbeam on my face
Lightly dusting my pillow
Too cold to get up.

Winter snap, such chill
But sunny days to follow
Seasons come and go.

Magpies in the trees
Warbling on a sunny day
Then the bulldozer

Frog on the lily
Carefree flies in the soft wind
Slurp!

Soft wind on my face
Facing east to the sun rise
Miracles happen

Rain drops on a leaf
Small gifts arrive every day
All is perfection

Helen

———

Fielding in the deep,
Smack of ball against willow,
Deluge. Rain delay.

Space lady to go,
Disappointment years ago,
Stars and moon still bright.

Fillet mignon done,
Appetising on table,
Phone rings. Dog runs.

With golden hues the
Autumn leaves covered the grass.
Whoosh! A blower cruel.

The scent so divine.
The colour more than vivid.
The thorn as a knife.

Geraldine

Barwarre Poets

Healing

This was written for a Barwarre Bush Poetry challenge where we were asked to create a poem using the words: Verandah; Golden Wattle; Mountain View; Magpies; Surrounding Scenery and Ghost gum.

Quietly minding my own business
on a deckchair on the verandah,
Having a smoke and thinking about
six blokes coming back from Uganda.

They went out there because of the tax,
big money but a pretty hard life.
I have distant memories of there
every day filled with trouble and strife.

I would rather be here on my farm,
golden wattle, the river and all.
That superb mountain view from my chair
peaceful silence, just the magpies' call.

Surrounding scenery is a balm
those six men will now feel they don't fit.
Some strong ghost gum healing I reckon
better get them up here for a bit.

Helen

Henry the Hungry Huntsman

Henry the huntsman was always hungry
already today he has eaten
three chickens, four dinosaurs and five elephants
but still his hunger he has not beaten.

When he hatched, he was pale and small
but each of his eight eyes shone so bright.
He had two hundred and forty-five siblings
all happy and wiggling, squashed up tight.

"Oh oh", he yelled, as he fell over,
"it's hard to walk when you have eight legs.
But it could be worse," he giggled, "I could be
a silly sailor spider with eight pirate pegs."

Wordwaves

Now Henry obviously likes his food
and he always asks for more.
He ate and ate and ate and ate and
when he grew up, he went to live in a grocery store.

"Yummy. Yummy. Food for my
tummy",
he said, and he spent all day and night,
gorging, gutsing until his tum was full.
He ate every single thing in sight.

He started with chips, jelly and jam,
all eight legs crammed food in.
"More. More", he cried,
as the food dribbled down his face and
chin.

Yum, yum", said Henry but
so great was that load
of food and stuff inside his tum
his tum it did explode.

"Oooops", said Henry, quite alarmed
as down the food did rain.
"What shall I do, I'm still hungry",
so he smiled and ate it all up again.

Tom

BARWARRE POETS

Homeless

This was a bush poem I wrote in 2019. It is a true story and one I often think about. Bush poetry seems quite regimented and the syllable requirement is a challenge, but I find I can sometimes produce something that meets the rules and yet tells a story and feels quite lyrical.

He knocked on the door and I answered,
he stood so dishevelled and beat.
I'm so hungry he told me and asked,
do you have any food I could eat?

He was a tall man, thin and bedraggled,
pale blue eyes in a face kind of grey.
Guess he'd not seen a bathroom,
or a good meal in many a day.

I was home alone at the time,
and afraid to let him come in.
So I told him to wait on the footpath,
he understood with a rueful half grin.

I went to the kitchen to look for
something to provide him a feed.
A sandwich with ham, cheese, tomato,
a mug of tea I thought he might need.

Not much but he thanked me and leaned
on the wall to eat but not fast.
He tasted and savoured it slowly,
Like he needed to make it all last.

I leant on the wall alongside him,
and asked how far he had walked.
The length and breadth of Carlton,
seeking food, and then he talked:

He told me a bit of his life,
t'was a sad tale indeed that he told,
a lost job, a dead child, a gone wife.
No family, no home and so cold.

Wordwaves

He sleeps rough in a railway culvert,
keeps a blanket or two in a swag,
rolled up and stuffed in a hollow.
Some clothes he keeps in a bag.

Best be moving along he then told me,
gave me back the plate and the mug
'Thanks love' and he shook my hand firm
and I wanted to give him a hug.

As he left, I felt so remorseful,
lacked the courage to bring him inside.
Find proper food, steak and some veggies,
A warm bath some fresh clothes beside.

Does anyone ever invite him in
to come right on in through the door
or like me are they frighened of something
of someone being more than just poor.

I guessed it is what he sees mostly,
when I told him he couldn't come in.
That resigned little shrug and a sigh,
and that small lonely rueful half grin.

What has brought me to this way of thinking?
Fear wins and humanity gets lost.
Compassion outweighed by suspicion,
and I think it was me paid the cost.

Deep down I knew he was harmless,
a poor man whose life fell apart.
I just wish that I'd had the courage
to really reach out from my heart.

Helen

I Was Autumn Once

Wordwaves

This poem is the result of me, at the age of fifteen, having to memorize and recite 'Ode to Autumn' by John Keats to a packed auditorium.

I was autumn once, dressed as a leaf
And full of 'mists and mellow fruitfulness' with no relief.
Ten minutes of cruelty I had to bear
Because the nuns decided I should share

The joys of 'ripe fruits and lambs' so grown
With a crowd of parents not want to moan
At speak of 'gourds or maturing sun.'
Autumn was of interest to everyone!

But much worse, a private beckoning to the parlour
By nuns so old but full of ardour
To hear of 'wailing gnats and clammy cells'
And the 'plumpness of some hazel shells'.

As I stood there I was 'borne aloft'
By a wind so strong yet strangely soft
To a place of a different feel and hue
Spring please save my saneness, do.

So when I finished with the ode
I bowed and smiled and quietly strode
away from all that was the season
Which brought to me no rhyme nor reason!

Geraldine

Just a Thought

I wonder should we write a tome
About Barwarre, which is our home
Oh what secrets we could tell
And I reckon such a book would sell

Crazy mad goings on we see
But should we tell, or silent be
We'd lose some friends of that be sure
And perhaps we'd be up before the law

Best we hold our tongues, leave all to the fates
Just enjoy our lives and keep our mates
No book, no fame and yes, no pay
Best just get on with the day

Helen

Memories of My Dad

I was looking through old photographs,
Grasping gossamer threads of memories,
Remembering things I had thought forgotten,
When my focus settled on my Dad.

A child of the Depression, he left school at twelve,
Had to get a job to help support his large family.
Rode a bike in all weathers delivering telegrams,
Got a job in a grocery store, worked his way up, studied hard.
I still have the certificates he earned in his trade.
Knew his duty, my Dad was a survivor.

WORDWAVES

He knew the pain of losing his first wife at the birth of his child,
The trials and danger of being a gunner in the Orkneys.
Then the joy of meeting his second wife, my Mum
On a blind date at that! Two more children to join the first.
Played board games, and card games, walked many country miles.
Loved us all, my Dad was a family man.

He worked his way up from deliveries to store manager
Could eye up and cut a wedge of cheese or butter with no scales
Heft a bag of sugar or flour in his hand and have correct weight,
Bone out a side of bacon, cut ham or beef wafer thin,
Knew all the prices and added up columns of figures in his head.
Sounds simple, but my Dad was a grocer.

He was a teller of tall tales, a master of words,
Did cryptic crosswords in a flash.
Took me to the museum and the library next door,
Helped me choose books and to read them while he read his.
I used to think he could do anything he put his mind to.
My clever Dad was a self-taught scholar.

So many memories of this down to earth man,
The outrageous stories he could tell with a straight face,
Endless songs that he made up as he went along.
He knew faith was important and took us to Sunday School,
Sang all the old hymns while he polished the shoes each week.
My very special Dad was an extraordinary man.

Sheila

Marlene

Marlene phoned, she's coming up
Make the coffee, fill the cup
Friendship always took the floor.
Conversation, we talked more
These good things we used to sup
How we kept the spirit up.

Friendship always took the floor
These good feelings, lots in store
Computer IT not our theme.
Good neighbours all, they joined the team
Now it's a nightmare, not a dream.

Marlene left us......... pained and shocked
Even left the door unlocked.
Tears and sadness, nothing mocked
Too soon Marlene........no more to dwell
How we wished a fond farewell.

Flowers, poems, paintings, books
Into these good things we looked.
Don't rely on 'certainties'
Today we lost a pal for sure
When we really wanted more.

Nancy

Medical Profession

There's the learned neurologist
and the amazing top urologist.
We learn from the cardiologist
and the eminent radiologist.
They chat, consult and spy
with the lung respiratory guy.

No I can't come out to play,
I've a specialist to see today.
Medical scientists all around,
they have thinking very sound.

Mostly folk are in remission.
They often see their smart physician.
We forever want the best,
so we go in for a test.
They want so many samples,
in no time we've produced ample.

To help with our recovery,
every day a new discovery.
We must thank the medical profession
for their super clever expression.

Nancy

Milk

Grandchild, I know you are besotted,
buying cow's milk in a bottle.
Give a thought to those who milk,
Nowhere else you see their ilk.
In this age now automatic,
You should never understate it.

Farming's uphill everyday
You will often hear me say.
Sometimes dry as chips or drier
Then the rain is sent to try us
Lots of mud it makes me cry.

We eat ice-cream when you come
Child, you never see me glum.
Cheese on toast and yoghurt too
Egg custard, all fruits to stew

Keeps you out of lots of strife
Keeps you riding on your bike.
As in life create the zest for it is the very best.
Just remember milk's a food
Don't try skim it's not as good.

At fine restaurants, real nice tucker,
Food you really like to succour
Wear stylish linen or your silk
Many dishes made with milk.
Fine chopped celery, cottage cheese
Apple pie with lots of cream.

Cock-o-leaky soup tureen
Chef's delight in dairy dreams
You need strategies and schemes.
You've got lots of stuff to do
Join the winning sports team true.
Milk builds strong minds, bodies too.

Nancy

Mother's Driving Adventures

We bought a car in Whyalla, our first one ever, brand new
Dad was one happy fellow, his pride a Corolla, bright blue.
Mother longed to drive that car, full of confidence, had no fear,
She'd never tried a car before, just played the dodgems on Brighton Pier.

Father thought he could do the job so he chose the road to Iron Knob
It was long and straight no bends to touch, he taught Mum the gears, to use the clutch.
The first few k's they were doing fine, but then came the curve by the railway line!
Mother turned the wheel but not quite enough
The next thing she knew they were into the rough.
A stobie pole looming she pressed on the brake
But her foot off the other she forgot to take!
Dad grabbed the wheel, and the car turned away
That was quite enough driving for Mother's first day!

The lessons continued, Dad's patience sublime
And Mother's confidence started to climb.
She drove to the shopping mall, down to the park
But her downfall came one night in the dark –
She'd practised her parking, she knew left from right.
But on coming home gave us all such a fright,
Her sense of direction being not too sweet
She tried to go UP a DOWN one-way street!

A baby bump came betwixt Mum and the wheel
Her legs were too short the pedals to feel
So for the time being she abandoned the quest
And gave brave Dad's lessons a very long rest.
When to Tassie we went Mum thought she would learn

Barwarre Poets

To drive the new Datsun, and then take a turn
On the school run, for outings, to go for a run
She really did think it would be lots of fun.

From Savage River Mum drove down the hill
Got to Luina and felt such a thrill.
Mastering hill starts, parking in a straight line
She set off for home thinking all was fine.
But the road was so steep and the bends so tight
Knew she had to change gear, slow down just right.
But to do that one hand had to let go the wheel!
Her foot hit the brake, the tyres started to squeal,
She shot round the corner and stopped with a yell
Her driving days finished it was plain to tell!

So, Mum never drove, caught a train or a bus
And her boys learned to drive without any fuss.
They added some grandchildren with us to stay
We took them to Warrnambool on holiday.
Those grandsons we took to Lake Pertobe
They asked for a motorboat ride.
Mum gave one the wheel but he said, "No,
He'd much rather sit alongside".
Well, he was so small and she was so stout
The boat tipped at an angle he nearly fell out!
She went round in circles just couldn't go straight
The boy grabbed the wheel, it was far too late.
Tight stuck in some bushes they just couldn't move
Then Grandad came past and gave them a shove.
Said Grandson, "Thank goodness we got back alive,
And now I know why my Gran doesn't drive!"

Sheila

My Friend Has Gone

My friend has gone
Not from a place, but from me.
Our shape was high and wide and deep with a distance of infinity.
It measured and forgave. It soothed and stretched.
Folding and unfolding, it understood.

Tumour or is that tumours?
Matters not. Wires crossed in cruel finality.

Geraldine

My Guts Are Gone

Oh no, my guts are not there.
They were here yesterday, I swear.
Something's horribly wrong.
I'm empty, washed out, not strong.

No, this can't be true,
Whatever will I do?
Yesterday I felt quite well
but today I'm just a shell.

Hang on, one of my legs is gone,
Did I lend it to Uncle Ron?
No, he doesn't need me that to do,
he's already got a spare or two.

What else is gone, I wonder.
Did it go as I did slumber?
Did something suck me dry,
as I did gaze upon the sky?

Guts can't just up and go
can they? Please say, No.
Work it out. Think. Think. Think.
Did I leave them in the kitchen sink?

Or perhaps I put them behind the door,
I have been known to do that before.
Maybe I ate my guts, as I sometimes do,
and pushed them out as thick brown poo.

Wordwaves

There has to be a sensible reason.
It's not yet gut-losing season.
Did I lose them in my tree?
Or cook them nicely for my tea?

Hang on, hang on. I do recall.
It is quite normal after all.
We spiders have our bones outside
and all the soft stuff squashed inside.

When we grow too big for our skin
we shuck it off, chuck it in the bin.
That's it, that's what I remember,
My guts have gone to something bigger.

I'd better hurry up and find them
for I have a great big problem.
My new body will not know what to do.
Guts do need a brain or two.

There they are. Hang on, you guys,
you need brains to control eight eyes.
Here I come. I'm almost there

SPLAT. SCRUNCH. SQUELCH.

Ooops. A sad interruption to our poem.
You know that spider? The one almost there?
Well, sorry but he got squashed on the second stair.

Tom

My New Chair

My new chair in my new place is different to my chair at home

It is brown leather, not cream linen

There is no down filling to sink into, and it hasn't a frame guaranteed for fifty years

But it allows me to get out of it like a teenager

I like my new chair in my new place

Geraldine

My Sewing Machine and Me

I pulled my sewing machine out today
To make a Covid face mask.
It's not what I'd choose I really must say,
I'd prefer another task.

My mind runs over the things that abound
Since Mother taught me to sew.
Pretty dolls clothes made from the scraps in her mound
Little peg dolls all in a row.

Moved on to my own clothes just to my taste
When I wanted to go into town.
None of Mum's fabrics was left to go waste
But the miniskirts made my Dad frown!

My own children wore things I had sewn,
Tops, shirts, pyjamas and pants.
I kept sewing until they were grown
And brand names came into their wants.

When friends found out my talents could stretch
Oh the things that they asked me to make!
From Nun's habits, to clothes they would sketch
Fancy costumes to make my head ache.

Wordwaves

So my list of accomplishments stretched with the years
My skills grew as the boys' lives progressed.
Wedding gowns for their brides caused some tears
But on their big days I felt really blessed.

The same sewing machine was still going strong
When seven grandchildren came into view.
The old patterns I had kept all along
Then came out to make something new.

And now a new generation has begun
As machine and I both grow old.
Sewing small things no longer seems like fun
Think I'll take them to where clothes are sold!

Sheila

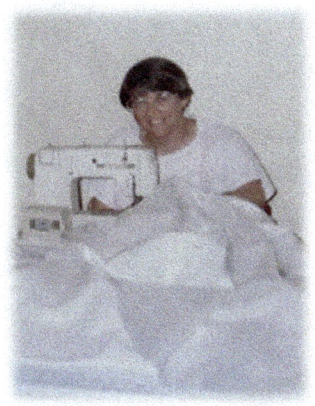

WORDWAVES

Naming Baby

Each with two tries, and stars in their eyes
They decided to add to their brood.
A girl would be great, but let's leave it to fate
To be greedy would be simply too rude.

The baby was born an hour close to dawn
A daughter the pair would be claiming.
An aunty or two, and a nanna named Sue
Held a breath in the wait for the naming.

Each secretly hid, a wish for the kid
To carry their name, like a pearl.
But it wasn't to be, 'cos the parents you see
Had chosen the one for their girl.

'Maggie Louise', drifted light as a breeze
To the ears of the parents so besotted.
To miss out on fame, would prove such a shame
The aunts and the nanna's hearts knotted.

They tried with the story, that ends without glory
About Maggie in the quest for its freedom.
The cow would jump fences, devoid of all senses
With a frequency heralding tedium.

But their minds were true, to no Sue or Prue
So to the parish without a regret.
The priest he did bless, with water no less
And baptised her after Saint MARGaRET!!!

Geraldine

Niente (Nothing)

A quiet heart, seeing loss in the mists ahead
Sitting by a window, thinking, feeling
Looking out to the garden, a small sigh

Small whispers in the trees, sharing
Thoughts of wisdom of the ages
'Nothing lasts forever'

'Nothing to be done', it draws to a close
Written in the annals of time
Her turn now, mine one day

Surrender is the goal, a quiet letting go
'Unbinding and leave-taking'
Words carried in the breeze through the trees

Nothing left to do, nothing to stay for
Wherever it got left, it is done
Someone else will finish it … Or not

There was a purpose, legacy left
Stretching not far into the future
Where it disappears

Wordwaves

Doesn't matter, purpose is in children
And friends and strangers
Who knows who we touch and how it counts

Sixty years, a long time but not long
Going no further now
It is almost done

Sitting by the bed, breath in – sending love
Breath out, taking pain
Hour after hour, in and out

Walking in the garden reflecting
Brevity, purpose and in the end
Nothing but love, and gentle care

Niente.

Helen

October

There's a wolf baying to the moon
In October the veils are thin
I feel the breeze of a spirit wafting by
And other-worldliness creeps in.

Breezes are significant to me
The gentle touch upon my face
I was told it is my mother
Come to hold me with her grace.

I have no memory of her at all
She died when I was only small
So I love the breeze and to know she's here
Maybe she'd come if I knew how to call.

I remain deeply afraid of the dark
But it is not the spirit world I fear
But human malevolence, always around
And the threat to the life I hold dear.

My mum is welcome any time
And dear friends and rellies who have passed
Come into my space and walk along side
Guide me through life with your wisdom vast.

Helen

Pebbles

I gaze up through the sparkling water
See the reeds at the edge of the creek
Tiny rainbow trout dart around me
Round behind me a frog takes a peek.

I've been here as long as forever
And I love when the clouds drift on by
Or the rain splashes into the water
I don't mind because I'm never dry.

Schools out and little Jimmy comes running
Boots off and he is in quick as a flash
He loves the sparkles of the sun on the water
Over the pebbles and he's got quite a stash.

He has picked me up now and then
But I'm just plain so I always go back
He likes us all stripey or shiny
And he doesn't like even a crack.

But I don't mind because I am happy
In my creek bed with all of my mates
His visits are always delightful
Being plain is just one of my fates.

But what's this, a giant metal scraper
And I am lifted right out of my home
And into another big metal thing
And I am shaken right through to the bone.

Barwarre Poets

Then tipped out with a roar and a rattle
And I am part of a pile on the ground
A strange place, quite foreign and lonely
And not a single drop of water around.

For three days I lay there abandoned
No fish, no frogs and no lad
Drying up and bereft and forsaken
Could anything ever be so bad.

But wait, bless my soul it is Jimmy
Lifting us all one by one
He presses me close to his cheek
And it feels like a touch of the sun.

He lays me down with the others
As the man sorts design with a flair
Then he digs holes along the side
And puts plants in with such tender care.

Soft ferns now sway about me
And they whisper everything is alright
This is Jimmy who lives with his father
You will see, it will all be quite bright.

They've made a dry creek bed with pebbles
All come from Jimmy's favourite place
Now he lies down beside me each day
And I feel I am blessed, touched with grace.

Wordwaves

He trickles water downhill that gathers
In a pool at the end of the line
There are goldfish there, I can hear them
And I think this place is just fine.

Now the old frogs have found me,
And there are lizards and birds every day
And Jimmy and his mates with their water games
All's well that ends well I say.

Helen

Relief

A fortnight of studied calm, swallowing our apprehension
As my friend had the tests and then we waited
Some unexpected pathology, located deep causing tension
Potentially sinister, so we didn't underrate it.

We didn't put into words the thing that we feared
Lest speaking aloud makes it true
But put paperwork in place as the appointment date neared
And let those know who should, just a few.

It lurks in your mind though despite attempts at blocking
It creeps into dreams dark at night
It takes work to not to give in to thoughts that are shocking
But to hope that it will all be alright.

Surgery they said so get ready,
get as well you can by this date
So she's on to deep breathing and work on her mind
While I walk alongside as a mate.

Then at last comes the specialist visit,
and we wait till she opens the door
'Good news' she says as she ushers us in
And immediately our hearts start to soar.

Driving home we stopped for some bubbles
Monday lunchtime notwithstanding
Got to celebrate when you discover that troubles
Are all now joyfully disbanding.

Helen

Rural Women's Network

Some years ago, the Government decided to publish a rural women's magazine.
The idea was to update us regarding services etc. In the next issue of OUR magazine they not only printed my poem but in the next issue, asked the readers,"What makes you laugh?"
I thought to myself, "that's the power of the pen at work!"
I was important enough for the Magazine to listen to me!

This is a poem I sent them.

Golly oh gosh and yippee
A magazine that's just for me
Believe or not it's even free.
Now I can go on a reading spree.
Women's Network, this I need
Send it again with plenty of speed.
I'll fill out the questionnaires with glee.
I'll need to know ethnicity
I'll read on health and well I'll be.
Cultural effects from poetry
Writing skills encourage me.
Memories of raising kids
Investigation into SIDS.

Barwarre Poets

Conferences I'd love to attend
How to make the budget bend?
Women's net-work staff
Lighten up, I need to laugh.
Bring a conference nearer to us
Make a fuss of important us.
Teach us how to lighten our load
Improve our skills in modern mode.
Learning things I need to know
Clears my brain, the line to toe.
Stimulate and keeps me bright
Helps me see the 'other light'.

Nancy

Seasons Come...

There's no doubt that the soil has become warmer
It's September so that's just about right
Today was for weeding, pruning, planting, feeding,
And I reckon tonight I'll sleep tight

There's a definite mood lightening in spring
Though I don't really mind winter's cold
It's extreme heat and gale winds I don't like
But really, any season's ok, truth be told

We Oz whities only have four seasons you know
And sometimes all in one day
But Indigenous Australia has so many more
So, I'm reading so I'll know the way . .

. . to read the earth so much better
And relate much more deeply to land
So, the birds, clouds and sea mists can teach me
And I'll be able to better understand

Helen

So, What Now...?

This was a fifth Covid lockdown thought. Coming out slowly in a hopeful kind of mood.

There is a spark that seems to have gone
Inspiration lacking
Is it Covid? Getting old
Or has my oomph gone packing?

I used to be just full of beans
With ideas and plans impatient
To get out, get going, just get cracking
But lately I seem complacent.

Seventy-four's not that old
My eighty five year old neighbour goes biking
Compared to her I'm slothful
Yet I do have the blood of a viking.

Wordwaves

Shake it up, stretch it out
Send inertia packing
Brisk walks and good fresh air
And make the joints stop creaking.

There's life in the old girl yet
I tell myself quite sternly
Determined to get going again
I say "get up", quite firmly.

So now there's walks and yoga,
and belly dancing slinky
and Irish drum and bongos
but nothing remotely kinky.

Post Covid, whatever that is
I'm waking in body and brain
With energy and interest now
I think I'm emerging sane.

Helen

Song for Ukraine

In shock and disbelief they gather
An enemy without
Sudden, brutal, shocking.

Tanks down the main street
Miles long convoys into the towns
Explosions, fire, devastation.

People run, white faced, bloodstained
Where to go, nowhere to hide
And still they come.

Solidarity, take up arms
Molotov cocktails, people power
Against the might of Russia.

Wordwaves

The might, but not the right!
A sovereign country
Peaceful, democratic, growing, flourishing.

Invaded while the world watched
Dismayed but standing back
Sanctions yes, guns no.

Grim faced, manning barricades
They watch and wait
They will not let them pass.

God hold them
Give them strength to endure
And prevail.

Helen

The Book

A swagman slumped sadly beneath a gum tree
And thought of his life as it used to be.
He'd had a fine home, a wife and a son,
But a bushfire had raged and now all were gone.

He went on the road to ease his pain,
Worked wherever he could for not much gain.
A roof for his head was all he would ask
He could mow, chop, fence, just about any task.

He headed down the old Wallaby Track
Carrying little but some clothes for his back.
Stopped off at an outback pub one day
He'd found enough cash for an overnight stay.

Wordwaves

He showered and shaved, lay down on the bed,
Was glad of a safe place to lay his head.
Idly opened the drawer to have a look,
Laying inside was a red covered book.

He started to read not quite knowing why
That the tale he read made him want to cry.
He read of a life lived long years ago,
This life showed our traveller a new way to go.

He discovered new purpose for his life ahead
He would tell other folk of the things he had read
Of love, joy, forgiveness and freedom from strife,
How all folk could choose for themselves this new life!

Our friend changed from swagman to preacher that day,
He blessed all the people he met on his way.
Their lives filled with joy as he taught from the Book
So glad he'd decided to take that first look.

From grief he'd been saved, a new life begun
He felt they'd be proud, his wife and his son.
And when the day dawned he could no longer roam
He heard a Voice saying, "Well done, now come Home".

Sheila

The Drop Spider

Look out for the scary Drop Spider.
She looks harmless, but there's a beast inside her.
Don't look up, she'll jump in your hair,
and eat guts or brain, she doesn't care.

Once she falls on top of your head
you'll quickly wish that you were dead.
She'll chomp your skull and munch your brain.
She'll crawl out your ear, you'll go insane.

Oh no, she is coming quickly.
I'm faint, frightened, scared and sickly.
Ah, she's here, I feel a leg, a leg,
Don't hurt me, please, please, I beg.

She's crawling now, right down my hair,
I'm watching with a cross-eyed stare.
I'm trembling in my clothes,
as she scuttles on to my nose.

Wordwaves

She stops and looks me in the eye.
as I prepare to say goodbye.
Her fangs are huge as up she goes
and gently kisses me on the nose.

"Tee Hee", she cried, "don't be afraid,
a silly mistake is all you've made.
Drop spiders are not really real.
I play this game to make you squeal.

Some people in their pants do pee,
but life is boring up a tree.
I'm sorry if I gave you a fright,
but a cup of tea will make it right."

Tom

The Literature Festival

The literature festival has been cancelled
Covid has interfered yet again
'Plan events lightly' so it was just pencilled
But it hurts and I still feel the pain

I was braving the train and the rain and the crowd
Booked a hotel and was ready to go
But that strong little bug's not the slightest bit cowed
It's riding high and so now there's no show

But where there's a will there's a way so they say
And some good ones have gone up on-line
I can listen and watch just as long as I pay
In my own time, in my home, with a wine

On line viewing is like a private tutorial
In my living room cosy and warm
An up close and personal pictorial
So familiar now it's almost the norm.

But I will miss the buzz of the festival
And the dozens of books I would buy
And the mood that is almost a carnival
I am resigned but I still give a sigh.

Helen

WORDWAVES

The Lobby

When I was 12, I lived at my grandmother's for a couple of years
and the house became special to me.
Years ago I wrote about the place. My Poem is based on a paragraph
from that piece of writing.

This room (Daisy's), together with a bedroom, bathroom and kitchen, opened onto a lobby, drab and dull, with dark brown oil-skin blinds shading the whole of one side.

But with its linoleum and darkness it was cool and when Christmas days sizzled with heat, the dinner would be transferred there. Miraculously the lobby would transform. The huge table with its ugly, faded, blood red cloth was covered with white damask. The red tassels fell beneat and when, in its centre, a mint green bowl, was filled with geraniums it would explode with the colour of Christmas.

It was easily the ugliest room - brown and dull and drab
But it was honest in its darkness and coolness with its slab
Covered in linoleum, with worn patches more than one
A place to get away from the blistering heat of the sun

And when that heat was such no man could race
The lobby in a whim would change its face
To graciousness with blood-red cloth cooled
By crisp white damask as if suddenly bejewelled

The large green bowl filled with geraniums red
Would sit amongst best crystal and silver instead
Of that of ordinary days which by necessity so much duller
For this was a special time, a time of Christmas colour.

Geraldine

The Mall Rats

Forget your 'roo, goanna and koala.
Of all the Aussie fauna and flora
none is greater than the humble Mall Rat.
Not even the maggie with his black hat.

The Mall Rat is an urban creature
and survival is its greatest feature.
It has endured through colonisation
as industry developed the nation.

The Mall Rat's ancestral line is as great
As brolga, wombat, eagle or snake.
It easily goes all the way back
on the Eureka resistance track.

Capital always needs the dispossessed
to do their dirty work while they do rest.
It is only when you create those 'out of luck'
that you can fleece them and make a buck.

Greed is what breeds the lean Mall Rat
and, scoffs the Toff, "you will never change that."
But the clever Mall Rats always adapt
banding together to avoid a trap.

The group, the tribe is all their strength.
To save the pack they go to great lengths.
Together they are accepted and sure.
Together they feel at home, safe and secure.

Wordwaves

All this Molly knew and understood.
All her life she was told she was no good.
But on the day she met the Rats, she felt
at home and her heart did melt.

She was not alone, there was a bloke, Bob,
a terrific guy, who once had a job.
But the Toffs closed the factory down
and he had to move away from town.

Since then life was a downward spiral
as he struggled to ensure survival.
His anger drove his wife and kids away.
His house went next as he further went astray.

Mary, with thoughts slow and limited skill,
felt she was always struggling uphill.
The Mall Rat community was her all.
As part of the tribe she was strong and tall.

But saddest of all were the young Ratlings.
Too sad, or slow or angry to know things.
One and all they fled home in fear and shame,
frightened until they took the Mall Rat name.

They wandered lost and lonely in the crowd,
trying very hard not to be too loud.
But how else can you be recognised
When all your life you have been despised?

The Merchants complain, whine and bleat,
"Please move them further down the street.
We're not making enough of a profit.
They're dirty, loud and won't stop it."

Barwarre Poets

The Council were in shock,
so they brought in Beethoven and Bartok.
These boys brayed and Bached but to no avail.
The Rats just slunk away leaving no trail.

When "Go and get Fugued" appeared on the ground
they knew a solution they had not found.
"Get a Handel on this", the people cried.
"We do not think you have really tried."

"Okay, bring out the heavy hitters.
Their scorn and hatred will move those sitters.
Come out Alan Jones from Bullies and Co.
With Andrew Bolt make these Mall Rats go."

Against Power and Hate the Rats could not stand.
They merged, they blended with the land.
"Our hides are tough, our skins are thick
We'll survive this push no matter how slick."

"Who are you to point the finger.
All we want to do is linger.
What once was common is now banned.
Give us back our public land."

So, I say, forget your sunburnt country
with its animals cute and cuddly.
For pure survival give me the Mall Rat.
In the urban jungle it knows where it's at.

Tom

The Room Belonged to Daisy

The house had many rooms. Daisy's was my favourite. She wasn't there any longer, but it was still referred to as 'Daisy's Room'. She had come from the orphanage when she was a girl of fourteen, to help, and had stayed until she married Les forty years later. Daisy was welcomed back as part of the family, and I remember when our visits coincided, her fierce hugs, the ample bosom and rough chin and the strong smell of talcum powder. Now her room was used for storage. Plums, apricots, peaches but mostly apples. Apples of every variety, stacked high. The smell was strong like Daisy, but sweet and crisp and clean.

    The room belonged to Daisy but now was spread
    With fallen fruit, apples galore where once a bed
    Had given respite at the end of frantic days
    Of washing, cleaning, cooking, often without praise.

    If you close your eyes the smell of cider crisp and clean
    Will waft across the asphalt quite unseen
    And bring the orchard's blossoms sweet in reams
    Of dizziness that will take you to her dreams.

Geraldine

The September Quake

There was an earthquake in Victoria this morning
I jumped up and ran out the door
The water in the birdbath was splashing about
My feet were not firm on the floor

I have studied the aftermath of floods
of fire and drought that brought dust
and I remember tremors that rattled the windows
but never did I ever lose trust

But when the ground that is under your feet
Shakes and shudders in ways you can't fathom
And there's nowhere to go and nothing you can do
Because the earth is twisting in spasm

It makes you wonder what to do
Get out of the house, that's the first
In case it all comes crashing down
Of possibilities that's probably the worst

It didn't last long, thirty seconds maybe
Not much damage and nobody harmed
So far a passing situation
And our lives this time were all charmed

Wordwaves

But I had a grandson on the mountain
Not far from the epicentre
So I rang my daughter and turned on the TV
And sat glued to the station presenter

He was up there in the snow
Ski classes for a qualification
Ski instruction and mountain guiding ambition
So this is all part of his education

All I could think of was avalanche
But it turns out he was always okay
The ski lifts were down but he is young and fit
So he just got on with the day

But it is a sobering reminder
We can think we're really in charge
But in the face of the power of nature
We are all just small fry, writ large

Helen

The WWW

This was part of Geelong Writers' Group challenge to mention 'Elephant' and 'Castle' in no more than one hundred words.

Dark.
Silence.
Spotlight.
Wrestling ring.
Ref calls for a clean fight.
Seconds out. The bout is on.
Elephant versus Castle.
Elephant is favoured: long trunk, four legs, mobile.
Elephant circles sandcastle.
Elephant trumpets, cocks a leg over the moat, pisses on the portcullis.
Castle oozes, a urine puddle.
Tusk half nelson, death drop from the ropes, castle sand everywhere.
Out for the count.

But wait. Elephant grimaces, sneezes. Sand invades every
grey crack, crevice, orifice.
Snuffled trunk. Gritty eyes.
Elephant slumps to the canvas.
She's down, she's out.
What a comeback.
Sandcastle.
WWW.
Weirdest Wrestler in the World.

Tom

There's a Gathering Sadness

There's a sadness in the air today
And it's wrought of many things
Like the soft grey mist that hangs in the trees
And the man who no longer sings

I shouldn't have read that book last night
The one that tells of you
I sat and wept for all those years
For it was my story too.

Helen

Barwarre Poets

The Times They Are a-Changin'

Change is an iceberg.
> Glistening, sparkling, shining.

> Pure, positive, promising more.

>> More equality.
>>> More diversity.
>>>> *More* opportunity.

Capital grows its inexorable march of power and prosperity.

Things are changing, and always for the better.

Even in the darkest dark
> the phosphorescent tip shimmers faintly,
>> a beacon lighting the way to better brightness.

It may be dark now, it seems to say, but dawn, *change* is coming.

Yes, my friend,
> here is good.
>> Now is noble.
>>> The future full of promise.

Yes, my friend, the times they are a-changin'.

Ah, yes, *the* times they are a-changin'.

Wordwaves

       More equality.
             More diversity.
                     More opportunity .

But the beacon, the tip of the iceberg,
             is anchored by immense weight below.

Impenetrable, impervious, anonymous, this darkness
    defines,
        delineates,
            decides,
                dictates,
                    directs.

Ah, yes, *they* say, the times are bright,
      but
         below
            is a broiling, brooding mass.

Ice blue promises.

Black bowels control.

Stay, here, for just a moment.

Pause.

Consider.

Barwarre Poets

What controls an iceberg?

What decides the when,
                      the what,
                                      the where,
                                                          the how?

The crystal tip?

No. That is decorative. Attractive illusion.

What controls?
        The darkness, of course.
                That dead weight below, the rotting corpse of yesterday.

After Dark, black bile flows from the Sky,
        blood spurting from a headless Chicken Little.

The tip is irrelevant, superfluous.

        The darkness. The weight. The power. The force. The control.

Ah, yes, the times they are a changin',
        but still our politicians cry "Stop shagging men"
                while their mates masturbate on women's desks
                      and share spilt seed on social media.

                Darkness. Weight. Power. Force. Control.

The darkness is the dismissal of the Uluru Statement from the Heart.

Wordwaves

                Darkness. Weight. Power. Force. Control.

In celebrations that female protestors "weren't met with bullets".

                Darkness. Weight. Power. Force. Control.

The *same* directing darkness in our obscene acceptance
        of the everyday deaths of women and First Nations' peoples

                Darkness. Weight. Power. Force. Control.

Ruby shoes might take you to Kansas, but they will not make you party leader.

                Darkness. Weight. Power. Force. Control.

The darkness anchors us,
        weighs us down,
                holds us down,
                        suffocates us

Ah, yes, my friend, the times they are a changin'.

Ah, yes, *the* . . . .

Tom

This Way or That

Pondering life's crossroads often has me bemused
So often a turning point, would I stand accused
If I chose this over that, would it lead to despair
A decision to be made, and to be made with all care

I said yes to this job, I said yes to that trip
I said yes to this man, could have given him the slip
it could all have been otherwise in the blink of an eye
And the map of my life by the roll of the die

I wonder how it might otherwise have been
different life, different me, different places I'd have seen
do I regret the path that I trod, cause it's not all been fine
Well, by choosing this over that I created my song line

Helen

Today

Today the lovely Kaye Morrison died
It feels difficult to believe
a vibrant, sunny kind of woman
whose loss we all will grieve

Today I won The Joker
Lots of money, lots of cheer
Fifth card on the corkboard
But it felt a little queer

Today turned into happysad
A disquieting kind of feeling
A dash of pleasure but all mixed up
With a loss that sent me reeling

She wasn't particularly a friend
But I feel a depth of sorrow
So today is kind of mistyblue
It may be yellower tomorrow

Helen

BARWARRE POETS

Trying Day

I really enjoy people and believe Life is like a smorgasbord with choices abounding. Sadly, sometimes I find it hard to make friends. I'm like Jonathan Livingstone Seagull. Jonathan was the seagull who effortlessly rode on the warm currents. He called to the other seagulls to make the extra effort and join him on the warm currents. They couldn't hear him, so he was left friendless.

What did I do today?
Read the "Addy", read the Sun
Fought the "war" but did I win?
Tried to smile, it's not a sin.
Was I kind to all and sundry?
Did I cross some social boundary?
Hob nail boots across some feelings.
Unintended, folk "cut and bleeding"?
Come up here, warm currents fine.
Jonathan Livingstone Seagull divine.
Take a leaf from his good book.
Make it easy, knock on wood.
Swooping down to catch a fish.
Lovely supper, it's delish.
Served with vegies so nutrish.
Tried hard, to win and yet.....
Go to sleep, sun's way past set.

WORDWAVES

Experience life and its storms.
Wake with vigour in the morn.
There's no way that I'm a saint,
I have no reason for complaint.
My body's up to speed,
I have everything I need.
The good Lord has not seen,
to send me all the shiny beads.
It is likely the trend,
I'm not meant to have a friend,
I've no need for this resentment.
He has sent me peace/contentment
So begone you trying day.

Nancy

Village Life

The decision to sell, to buy somewhere else
Is huge
Packing up a lifetime, what should stay, what should go
And why
Reliving old memories, happy times and sad
And then we leave.

And unpack in a new place, carefully chosen
Hopeful.
Chosen for convenience, for safety, for companionship
Been lonely.
And what now, unpacked, stuff sorted, I look around me
What now?

Go out and meet people, say hello, find a tribe.

Helen

Violence

And then there is me, tra la la la lee
My hair's all curls, my dress is a swirl.
I walk with a swing, my sandals are bling,
I hear a Jazz song I'm going to sing.

I would not have stopped, but then I turned back
I thought her ugly, just dressed in a sack.
One eye askew, the other was black
The poor thing had suffered a most terrible whack.

I stood transfixed, my heart was licked
My feeling turned to liquid mist.
A shift of thought, outside my wish
This type of thing's not on my list.

What can I do to mend this woe?
There are people whose bruises don't even show.
Is there something here, we don't know
Insults, put downs, lies, more woes?

I know that I will shed more tears
Certainly, I'm listening, with both ears.
About the insults and out-right sneers
Can we rebuild your life, your career?

The bullies who bellow, I pity too,
Results are the pits, this I cannot chew.
Male, female, all my sympathy
It would have to be the worst symphony.

Whatever happened to loving and kind,
It's patently obvious, their loss of mind.
How to rebuild these torn shabby lives,
Firm foundations, one brick at a time?

I'll cook some vegies, bake a few scones
I'll give it one flick of my magic wand.
I've learned it's worthwhile
To give friendship and love with a smile.

The smart experts say, don't ever go back
It just isn't worth another attack.
Why risk it all, it's so absurd
Next time it could really be murder.

I know you recall, a joyful December,
It felt just right, you'll always remember.
You fell in love, no time for tears
Then came that fateful moment, full of fear.

Your love was torn by a monster shove
A sad end to your true love.
To begin a new life, find the real you,
Seek old friends and new, go for counselling too.

After receiving that terrible assault
You said, "it was really my entire fault".
It is not your fault, you deserve better
Use good sense, write a stiff legal letter.

Nancy

Voice in Tribute

These poems were written after the Ash Wednesday bushfires in 1983. I wrote them to go into my PhD thesis when I could not find anything that really expressed what I had seen and heard. My thesis was about recovery in the aftermath of that fire in the Great Ocean Road area of Victoria.

Omens

Searing heat, made of wind and flames,
unknown, unseen but suspected.
Mothers gather their young and dread the parting.
They know the signs that bind the men to the work.

The beach is cooler, waves lapping idly
as though a world away from the nature-sister nearing.
They hover, reluctant to leave the water
fearful of the lull.

They've seen it all before, and the dogs and birds are restless.
There can be no mistake. A deep breath
and on to the task.

Barwarre Poets

My Patch of Dirt

You know, he didn't have a hope.
What did he think of in those last seconds as he ran,
his youth?
his wife?
his life?
not to **be** much longer?

Was he scared?
He was so determined;
our patch of dirt
our land
our sacred space.

We'll never know
anything
but the courage.

Earth Soul

How can it ever heal?
the burn scars sear so deeply.
It's as though the gods have thundered
down a wrath to hurt so keenly.

The little clearing by the fence
where wild geese flock for water
where kangaroos and magpies come
has turned from home to slaughter.

When nature wounds itself so much
how hard it is to know
that struggle is the food of soul –
a teacher, not a foe.

The Cairn

Up on a ridge, behind the forest,
they buried it all.
Deep holes, heavy earth moving machinery,
they covered it up
forever.

Someone said there ought to be a cairn,
something to mark the spot
of pain,
and loss.

A whole town lies buried there,
charred, melted fragments.
All the hopes,
the history, the memories,
gone.

There is no marker but it doesn't matter.
The people know where it is
and the land is sacred.

Helen

Water Runs Downhill - Part 1

i am a drip
lets go lets go go
theres no time to be slow
on our never-ending trip

whats next what now
so far Ive come down
glistening like a crown
whats that its called a cow

it must like me
its stooping to drink
it tickles as i shrink
i love its hooves pats and pee

well wheres the sun
come on out and shine
give us a sunny sign
being a pond is no fun

wow lovely heat
i feel better warm
i want to change my form
oh my god this is so neat

upwards we go
were starting to change
weve hit a mountain range
what will we be rain or snow

Barwarre Poets

golly gosh gee
this is cool and cold
worth a fortune in gold
who wants something else to be

although Ive been
up down and around
even part of the ground
still life has not lost its sheen

i cannot wait
to see what is next
no i dont want to rest
my desires ill never sate

what we are stuck
in a dirty puddle
a horrible muddle
to me its a matter of luck

for we can sing
and slosh and scream
one big watery team
making all of heaven ring

thanks to fates kiss
my whole life will be
a glorious journey
of eternal grace and bliss

Tom

Water Runs Downhill - Part 2

A life of bliss?
Smashed by a welly?
Tortured in the belly?
This life I would never miss.

Poor Prometheus?
Rolling a rock up a hill.
To see it roll down and stop still.
I don't understand all the fuss.

Okay, he did have it tough.
But really, he just upped and downed
while me, I go around and around.
Dizzy, sick and tired, I cry "Stop. Enough."

Here I go, down a hill, hit a farm gate.
Sit, smelly, for days and days and days,
crying, begging for the sun's stupid rays.
For God's sake. Come on. I'm tired of the wait.

Hooray. Yahoo. Up through the air we rise.
Higher, higher, until we get so cold
we have to hug together, young and old.
Shivering. Shaking, whimpering pitiful cries.

Overwhelmed, overweight, we spread and sag
until, with a scream and a shriek, we tumble.
Down. Down. Down. Down with a boring, rushing rumble.
Bang. Splash. Splutter. Oh no, we've landed on a sheep's dag.

A glorious journey of eternal bliss?
Always prodded from behind, below and above.
Far from a glorious journey of Fate's care and love
for this life I wouldn't give a rat's ass kiss.

Tom

Who Am I?

Did you decide from my writing who I am?
Do I write gospel, or is it a spam?
Am I scoundrel or a criminal in the slam?
Do you really know me, who I am?
No wonder they say that the pen has power.
So when I'm writing, I'm the 'man' of the hour!

Am I kangaroo an elephant or a lamb?
How could you know me when I don't know who I am?

I write to entertain, I'm amazed, you buy?
For you, reading is therapy, escape and a sigh.
For me writing is therapy, escape and a sigh.
It's stimulating, adventure for us both
Why don't we marry, or would you prefer elope?

Nancy

World Poetry Day

Exciting evening, we're out on the tiles
Modern library destination, we arrive
We glide to level five, and wander outside
Warm misty evening, a spectacular sight.
This pretty city our eyes to delight.
This autumn, Geelong city is painted in gold
Tourist from afar see a sight to behold.

 Ceiling is concave, this new building high domed,
As you would expect, it's nothing like home
Lined with large orange, reflective gloss squares
The lighting amazing, triangular and spare
Just leave me to ponder, I want to stare.

I sit in the front seats and hope I can hear
If I sit up the back, question marks may appear
I hope they speak, into the microphone
Hearing is a problem; in this I'm not alone.

Acknowledgement of Country, first poets of the land
Aboriginal culture we need to expand
Official memoirs and more, beautifully told.

Here alone, I'm a hick from the sticks
Like a fish out of water I don't socially click.
I really like fashion, sleek, pretty and all
The people are lovely, so slim and so tall.

Barwarre Poets

Not one sparkling diamond, not one glossy bead
Are my eyes focused, am I on speed?
The fashions so down beat, but studied and fine
My bright colours, way out of line.
I'll have to spruce up, I'll take a lend
Moth-eaten bank balance, I'll need to spend.

Award winning poets, stand to perform,
Not one word is rhyming, I'm startled I'm shocked
I'll have to take cover, I'm startled so mocked
This is Poetry with no rhyming chord?
Nowhere a rhythm, not sure I'm sold.

Words mingle and glide, an encouraging sign.
Words tumble down like a high water slide
Words so romantic, I begin to enthral
Now I understand, I am having a ball.

So.... un-rhyming poems, are they bone-fide?
And..... if there's no rhythm. I don't have to hide?
I thought.... poem rules, they don't exist?
Can I write as I please, I don't need to desist?

We're out on the terrace, the lights twinkle bright
Thank you Geelong, this is such a great sight.
So magic evening, fair thee well and good night.

Nancy

Yesterday

Yesterday I fell flat on my face,
showing a complete lack of grace.
It's not unusual for that to happen
since I'm 82 and close to heaven.

My nose is cut, my eyes are black.
How did I finish up on my back?
The staff here are so warm and kind.
This home has been a wonderful find.

Yes, I am sore. My skin is torn,
but, oh, that lovely sun in the morn.
I sit in the corner of my room,
as it seeps deep, deep into this dark little tomb.

Yesterday, my daughter Jenny visited.
She is so beautiful, strong and spirited.
We talked of Dad, kids, times gone past.
But the time, oh, it went so fast.

Things are quiet and calm and slow.
I see . .I see. . . someone I know?
Any time I want I can go
and see her, what's her name, you know?

Barwarre Poets

Yesterday I had a visitor, a bitch, hard and cruel,
bossed me around as if I was an old fool.
Shocked, in tears, saying she was my daughter Jenny.
Jenny, Jenny, oh, my poor stillborn child.

Yesterday they say I had a bad fall,
but today I bounced back, like a ball.
I wish someone . . . Where is that shoe?
I wonder what time my meds are due.

Yesterday, I . . . I . . . , I . . . what?
Yesterday, I . . . I . . .
Yesterday, I . .
Yesterday

Tom

Did you notice the italics in *The Times They Are a-Changin'*?

www.ingramcontent.com/pod-product-compliance
Lightning Source LLC
Chambersburg PA
CBHW050653160426
43194CB00010B/1919